C000044056

Following the Light of Christ

A practical guide on the way to God

Berthold Pelster

First Edition 2005
Text by Berthold Pelster
Cover illustration © Bradi Barth 2006
All rights reserved
© Aid to the Church in Need

ISBN 10: 0-9553339-1-1
ISBN 13: 978-0-9553339-1-0

In search of treasure…

So, you're looking for faith – the kind that can move mountains. You long for a future filled with hope. You yearn for a life filled with beauty and love. Does that make you a daydreamer? Maybe, but you're not about to give up your search for this treasure…

Well, this book might help you, like a guidance system in your search for this treasure. Try it – countless people before you have discovered the gift of an immortal hope through faith in Jesus Christ. And as for love, the Christian faith sees a close link between love of God, love of neighbour, love of our enemies and love of oneself.

Whether this is your first contact with the Catholic Church or whether you already share her life, maybe this simple handbook will be of benefit to you – a real treasure, we hope.

Why is this little booklet being offered by a charity that works internationally on behalf of persecuted, oppressed and suffering Christians? Father Werenfried van Straaten, the late founder of Aid to the Church in Need, saw himself as a shepherd of souls. His first aid projects in 1947 were for the suffering civilians in a defeated post-war Germany. The charity became a "gathering place of the Universal Church, where God's children from every nation on earth could meet and mutually enrich one another in supernatural love". His underlying goal was to fulfil Christ's double Commandment – to love God and our neighbour.

Let us begin our search, always following the star of happiness, just like the Three Wise Men on the front cover.

Your ACN team

The life pursuit

Today more than ever, the pursuit of happiness dominates our lives. Material gain – good food, a large house, exotic holidays – seems to be the ultimate aim in this modern age. But however much we have, there is always something else we desire.

> *He who loves money will not be satisfied with*
> *money; nor he who loves wealth, with gain:*
> *this also is vanity.*
> *(Eccles 5:9)*

Pleasure at any price

Whatever our tastes, there are always new pleasures to be sought, and new thrills to be experienced, no matter what the cost is. We leave no avenue unexplored in our quest to live life to the full – and sometimes we are so busy having fun that we put our own enjoyment ahead of our friends and loved ones.

> *And whatever my eyes desired I did not keep*
> *from them; I kept my heart from no pleasure.*
> *(Eccles 2:10)*

Living life to the full

We only get one chance at life and such is our desire not to miss out on anything, we often find ourselves too busy to worry about problems we may have in our lives – health problems, money worries, trouble at work, relationships on the rocks. There is no time to stop and think about things too deeply – life is too short! And suddenly our lives have sped along their course, and all too quickly they are over.

> *For man does not know his time. Like fish which are taken in an evil net, and like birds which are caught in a snare, so the sons of men are snared at an evil time, when it suddenly falls upon them.*
> *(Eccles 9:12)*

Searching for more

Even so, sometimes a strange feeling of uneasiness wells up in us. Despite our best efforts to ignore it, it grabs hold of us and refuses to let go. And we find our minds contemplating more and more that nagging question: "Surely this can't be all there is to life? There must be something more, something else?"

> *For all his toil, his toil under the sun, what does man gain by it?*
> *(Eccles 1:3)*

"Vanity, all is vanity"

Maybe you know this feeling of 'inner emptiness', when all your work and striving and enjoyment of life somehow brings you no real peace in the end – least of all when your plans, hopes and dreams are left unfulfilled.

> *Vanity of vanities, says the Preacher, vanity of vanities! All is vanity.*
> *(Eccles 1:2)*

Restless hearts

From time to time you may have had the feeling of a restless heart within you. Ask yourself if this inner restlessness has a reason, a cause – or more specifically, a Primary Cause.

Could it be God? Could it be your Creator, who made you and called you into being?

> *You have made us for yourself, O God, and*
> *our hearts are restless till they rest in you.*
> *(Saint Augustine)*

Your inner restlessness will only find peace when you finally get to grips with the idea that you have been created, and are loved, by God, your Maker – and when you make this truth the central message of your life.

Love responding to love

So maybe the yearning you feel within is in fact merely the echo of another yearning – the yearning of God for you. So is this experience in actual fact *your* response to the love that God has for you?

> *The longing of God is the living man.*
> *(Saint Augustine of Hippo)*

The theme of this book is that you are made by God and made for God. Nothing on this earth can ever satisfy this immense longing within. Only the infinite God can do so. Only in God can you find your true happiness – and in him you will find it with absolute certainty.

The entire earthly world can no more satisfy a soul that was made for God than a dusting of flour on a fingertip can satisfy a starving man. (Saint Jean Marie Vianney, the Curé of Ars)

Made for happiness

God, through his Holy Spirit, the Spirit of Creation, has made your human soul and called it to life. You have been invited into the Kingdom of God to live there for ever with God in absolute happiness.

And so your earthly life has been given to you in order to prepare you for this Eternal Life. God's Holy Spirit longs to accompany you on this path and desires to shape and form your soul, within the lifetime allotted to you, and so make it ready for life in the world to come. This is the plan that God has for your life. This is the deepest meaning of your life. This is your life's mission – to find the way that will lead you to God.

False lights

The longing that you feel within yourself has been put into your heart by God, your Creator, in order to lead you towards your life's goal. It is like an internal compass that points you in the right direction, like the light of a star that shows you the way.

Unfortunately though, especially in today's world, there are many, many false lights that seek to lead you astray. They tempt you along false paths and will never lead you to the goal of your deepest longing.

Take your longing seriously!

And so one of the most important things you can do in your life is to be aware of this deep longing within your heart, to listen to it and to learn to understand it, to seek out its mystery and follow it back to its origins – and so find God!

Don't let this inner longing fade away! Listen to it! It is the most precious thing within you! Pay attention to it and direct it on its true path. It must become a 'holy longing' that no longer leads you astray.

Following the star of longing

So, discover this star of longing within you; it will lead you to the true goal of your life. And then follow it, just as those Wise Men did two thousand years ago, when they set out on a long journey to follow a star – because they believed it was important and that it would lead them to a 'newborn King':

> *Now when Jesus was born in Bethlehem of Judea in the days of Herod the king, behold, wise men from the East came to Jerusalem, saying, "Where is he who has been born king of the Jews? For we have seen his star in the East, and have come to worship him." And lo, the star which they had seen in the East went before them, till it came to rest over the place where the child was. When they saw the star, they rejoiced exceedingly with great joy; and going into the house they saw the child with*

Mary his mother, and they fell down and
worshipped him.
(Mt 2:1-2; 9-11)

The wise men from the East were stargazers, who had come from far away to "pay homage" to this "new-born king of the Jews". They adored him and gave him rich gifts. Did they already glimpse something of the divine secret of this "King"?

God becomes Man – in Jesus Christ

But when the time had fully come, God sent
forth his Son, born of woman.
(Gal 4:4)

God's longing for communion with man is immense, and so "when the time had fully come", God himself became Man in order to be close to us in a quite special way, for the space of a human lifetime, and so to invite us into the Kingdom of God. He sent his own son, Jesus Christ, through whom we are able to know God better than ever before:

No longer do I call you servants, for the
servant does not know what his master is
doing; but I have called you friends, for all
that I have heard from my Father I have made
known to you.
(Jn 15:15)

Jesus called his disciples his 'friends'. Yes, God really does desire this friendship with us, his creatures! Through Jesus Christ we know this now – at last.

Becoming a friend of God

If you decide to accept God's invitation to friendship – and there is nothing more meaningful that you could do in your life – then you must turn to Jesus Christ. Become a friend of Jesus Christ. Become a friend of God!

But when you do, remember that we Christians believe in God, the Three-in-One. In a mysterious manner that surpasses our human understanding, the One and Only God contains within himself three divine Persons – God the Father, God the Son and God the Holy Spirit. We can learn to develop a deep relationship of friendship with all three divine Persons, while always being aware that this is the One and Only God.

Recognising God in Jesus Christ

The first step towards friendship with God is to know Jesus Christ better, to become familiar with his words and deeds. God became Man in Jesus of Nazareth in order that we might have a better understanding of who God is. Through Jesus Christ, God spoke to us in a human way.

> *No one has ever seen God; the only Son, who is in the bosom of the Father, he has made him known.*
> *(Jn 1:18)*

In Jesus Christ you will find the way to true life, the truth about real life, and finally, everlasting, eternal Life itself.

> *Jesus said, "I am the way, the truth, and the life; no one comes to the Father, but by me".*
> *(Jn 14:6)*

Getting to know Christ

The most important words and deeds of Jesus Christ have been written down in four separate Gospels.

Get to know these writings. Perhaps you could begin with St Mark's Gospel. It is the shortest of the four. It has sixteen chapters. If you read one chapter each day then, in just a little over two weeks, you will already know the most important things about Jesus. After that you could read St Luke's Gospel, and then perhaps St Matthew and St John. You should also read the Acts of the Apostles, and the letters of the Apostles. Then begin again from the beginning! In this way you will get to know the whole of the New Testament better and better.

Perhaps you can manage to seek this encounter with Jesus regularly, in the words of the Holy Scriptures – even if only for a few minutes a day. For it is your personal encounter with the longing of God, made Man in Jesus Christ.

The Bible – no 'easy read'

The Bible is not always an easy book, and nor are the Gospels either. Much is easy to understand, but other parts can be quite hard work at first. God understands our difficulties, however. And Jesus Christ has promised to help his disciples and friends:

> *But the Counsellor, the Holy Spirit, whom the*
> *Father will send in my name, he will teach you*
> *all things, and bring to your remembrance all*
> *that I have said to you.*
> *(Jn 14:26)*

It was only with the help of the Holy Spirit that the Evangelists, the writers of the Gospels, were able to set down their accounts of the life of Jesus. Likewise, it is only with the help of the Holy Spirit that we too can achieve a true understanding of the Gospels, and indeed of the whole Bible.

The Holy Spirit will help

That is why it is so important, every time you read the Holy Scriptures, to begin with a short prayer for guidance. Here is a short and simple prayer (suited to many other occasions too):

> *O God come to my aid! O Lord, make haste to help me!*
> *(Based on Psalm 70)*

Or you could turn directly to the Holy Spirit for help:

> *... Come, Holy Ghost, Creator, come, from thy bright heavenly throne. Come, take possession of our souls, and make them all thine own.*
> *(A hymn, based on an ancient 9th Century prayer by Rabanus Maurus)*

A little knowledge helps

Jesus Christ lived two thousand years ago. At that time many things were different from our own day. Jesus was a Jew and his life was completely imbued with the Jewish religion. He lived in a country that was under occupation by a foreign power, the Romans. Many of the things said and done by Jesus and those around him simply cannot be understood without further study. That's why there are guides to the Bible which explain such things and improve our understanding. Perhaps you too would find it helpful to glance through such a guide to the Bible.

Ask a Catholic priest. He will be able to recommend a good guide book. You can also look at one of the Catholic newspapers, which often have articles about that Sunday's gospel. Try it, and see if this helps you to improve your understanding of God's Word in the Holy Scriptures.

Those who have ears should listen

As you can see, to read and understand the Holy Scriptures requires a certain amount of effort and concentration. You need to practise listening to the Word of God. It doesn't always happen immediately, but usually requires some practice, some training.

> *Listen, who has ears!*
> *(Mk 4:9)*

It is also possible to listen without properly hearing, to see without really understanding (see *Mk 4:12*). So you need to train your senses, your eyes and your ears so that you can get beneath the surface and understand at a deeper level. God has given you a 'spiritual sense' so that you can see, hear and feel the divine. But your senses do not function automatically; you need to train them, to exercise them, and so gradually unpack the underlying spiritual meaning.

Good seed needs good soil

In the parable of the sower (*Mk 4:1-9*), Jesus is speaking about listening to the Word of God. He compared this Word with the seed that a farmer sows and which falls on different kinds of soil. Jesus himself explains this parable (Verses 15-20):

> *And these are the ones along the path, where the word is sown; when they hear, Satan immediately comes and takes away the word which is sown in them.*

> *And these in like manner are the ones sown upon rocky ground, who, when they hear the word, immediately receive it with joy; and they have no root in themselves, but endure for a while; then, when tribulation or persecution arises on account of the word, immediately they fall away.*

> *And others are the ones sown among thorns; they are those who hear the word, but the cares of the world, and the delight in riches, and the desire for other things, enter in and choke the word, and it proves unfruitful.*

> *But those that were sown upon the good soil are the ones who hear the word and accept it and bear fruit, thirtyfold and sixtyfold and a hundredfold.*
> *(Mk 4:15-20)*

And so you must devote time to the Word of God, you must stick with it and not be "rootless" and "fall away" (Verse 17). Likewise, you must not allow "the cares of the world" to "choke the word" (Verse 19). Instead you must "welcome" the word and receive it deep within yourself, like the rich soil. And like the soil, you must let the word rest in you, in your heart. Then, after a time, it will germinate in you and "bear fruit" (Verse 20).

Hearing – believing with all your heart

When one of the scribes asked Jesus what was the most important Commandment, he replied:

> *The first is, 'Hear, O Israel: The Lord our God, the Lord is one; and you shall love the Lord your God with all your heart, and with all your soul, and with all your mind, and with all your strength.'*
>
> *The second is this, 'You shall love your neighbour as yourself.' There is no other commandment greater than these.*
> *(Mk 12:29-31)*

Once again we are told to "hear". And it is a matter of all or nothing – when we believe in God we must do so with all our heart, all our soul and all our understanding, and we must commit ourselves to him with all our strength. It is a question of the highest form of love, the love of God.

And so your friendship with God must be 'wholehearted' – must spring from the very core of your being, from your *heart*.

Your *soul* is the place of encounter with God. It was created for communion and friendship with God.

But your faith in God can also hold its ground before human reason; it is something that must also be fully grasped by your *mind*. There is nothing irrational, nothing unreasonable about it.

Finally, this faith in God is something that demands your total commitment, your wholehearted engagement, all your *strength*.

So therefore the love that will come as the 'fruit' of this relationship with God must then characterise all your other relationships – both with yourself and with your neighbour.

Lean times

Of course, there will be times when you have no desire to devote yourself to the word of God. When this happens, you should try to overcome this feeling by asking God himself to inspire you with a new desire for his Word.

Among the people of Israel there was once a prophet, Amos, who was sent by God to the people to rebuke them for their social and economic misdeeds. These had come about because many people were no longer observing the Commandments of God. Amos made the following promise to them:

> *"Behold, the days are coming," says the Lord*
> *God, "when I will send a famine on the land;*
> *not a famine of bread, nor a thirst for water,*
> *but of hearing the words of the Lord."*
> *(Amos 8:11)*

You too should beg God to fulfil this promise! Ask him, implore him, to send you this hunger for the words of the Lord. Pray that this promised day of hunger for God may come about, especially in our own day. (It is well worth reading right through the Book of Amos at some time. In stirring words, the prophet calls for social justice because this is the will of God. It is a book of enduring topicality. This would be a good place for you to begin reading one or two of the books from the Old Testament too.)

Living God's Word

Although there is much in the Bible that is difficult to understand – and will long remain so – there is also much that is easily understood. So try to incorporate what you have understood into your daily life.

> *"Live whatever you have understood from the Gospel. No matter how little that may be... But do live it!"*
> *(Brother Roger of Taizé)*

In the first chapter of St Mark's Gospel, we have a very brief description of the way Jesus prayed:

> *And in the morning, a great while before day, he rose and went out to a lonely place, and there he prayed.*
> *(Mk 1:35)*

"A great while before day..." – there are two things we can learn here. First that Jesus takes the time, before any of the activity of the day, to converse with his heavenly Father, and second, that he seeks a place that is silent and apart. And so we too need to set aside a special time and find a quiet place for prayer.

Here is another example. The Evangelist St Luke tells us in Chapter 19 of his Gospel about the tax collector, Zacchaeus:

18

He entered Jericho and was passing through.
And there was a man named Zacchaeus; he
was a chief tax collector, and rich. And he
sought to see who Jesus was, but could not, on
account of the crowd, because he was small of
stature. So he ran on ahead and climbed up
into a sycamore tree to see him, for he was to
pass that way. And when Jesus came to the
place, he looked up and said to him,
"Zacchaeus, make haste and come down; for I
must stay at your house today." So he made
haste and came down, and received him
joyfully. And when they saw it they all
murmured, "He has gone in to be the guest of
a man who is a sinner."
(Lk 19:1-7)

Here you can learn that if you really want to see Jesus, to take an interest in him and get to know him – and are willing to make some effort to do so (like Zacchaeus climbing up into the tree), then you may be sure that Jesus will see and respond – he will notice you and come to you and want to "stay at your house" too. And don't imagine you are too small, too insignificant. For Zacchaeus was a "small" man in many respects – a dubious character, a tax collector who had doubtless cheated and abused many of his fellow Jews. He was a real sinner, and a figure of contempt, certainly in the eyes of the others. And yet despite this – or perhaps precisely because of it – Jesus chooses to be his guest.

And Zacchaeus stood and said to the Lord,
"Behold, Lord, the half of my goods I give to
the poor; and if I have defrauded any one of
anything, I restore it fourfold."

*And Jesus said to him, "Today salvation has
come to this house, since he also is a son of
Abraham. For the Son of man came to seek
and to save the lost."*
(Lk 19:8-10)

Maybe you too will find, in your own personal encounter
with Jesus, that there are many 'dubious' things, many
things that are wrong in your own life. Maybe, through
this same encounter with Jesus, you will find the
discernment, and above all the strength, to change those
things in your life that do not sit well with being a friend
of God. And so, you too can become a true "son (or
daughter) of Abraham". For Abraham is honoured as our
"father in faith", as the great example of the man of faith
and friend of God.

*"Abraham believed God, and it was reckoned
to him as righteousness"; and he was called
the friend of God.*
(Jas 2:23)

Learning from others

Look through the Bible for figures you can imitate, people
you can identify with, characters who perhaps share some
similarities with you (both in good and in bad things) and
observe how they responded to God, how they lived out
their friendship with God.

Solomon and an "understanding mind"

Take the young King Solomon, for example. God appears
to him in a dream and asks him what wish he would like to

see fulfilled. Solomon, who will later be renowned for his wisdom, answers:

> *Give thy servant therefore an understanding*
> *mind to govern thy people, that I may discern*
> *between good and evil.*
> *(1 Kings 3:9)*

You too should ask God for an "understanding mind" every time you sit down to read his Sacred Scriptures.

Sitting at the feet of the Lord, like Mary

Saint Luke's Gospel tells us of Mary, the sister of Martha,

> *"who sat at the Lord's feet and listened to his*
> *teaching".*
> *(Lk 10:39)*

Translated into daily life, this means that whenever you read the Bible you should do so always with the image of Jesus before your eyes. There are numerous widely varying depictions of Our Lord, and for centuries artists have endeavoured to portray the mystery of Jesus Christ in their pictures. You will doubtless have seen icons representing Jesus. Perhaps you could get hold of a simple postcard with an image or icon of Jesus on it. Then you could keep it close to your Bible whenever you read it. Or maybe you have a small crucifix with the figure of Christ on the Cross that you could sit before as you read and meditate on the words of Christ.

Not made by human hands

One image of quite special significance and impact is the cloth known and revered by many Christians as the 'Holy Shroud' or 'Turin Shroud'. According to tradition, this is the burial cloth in which the body of Jesus was shrouded, until the mysterious moment of the Resurrection. At this moment, when the body of Jesus was transformed to 'new life', his features were in an inexplicable manner 'burned' into the linen cloth.

Mystery of faith – condensed into the face of Christ

The face of Jesus Christ on this shroud can be seen as a summary of the entire Gospel. For the Son of God became Man in Jesus Christ and gave us the gift of his presence and love. He healed the sick, sought out the lost and invited all into the Kingdom of God, which had come close to them in his own person. Many people welcomed this Good News and believed in it. Others, however, rejected the invitation of God and many even sought Jesus's life. But he continued, undeterred, and went on proclaiming the news that the Kingdom of God was close at hand – a Kingdom in which justice and mercy, love and true peace would prevail and in which we are called to show love even to our own enemies. It was by the power of this love that Jesus was able, and willing, to remain faithful to his mission and to the will of the Father. So he had the strength to respond to the menacing, deadly violence only with gentleness and forgiveness. His love for his fellow men attained its perfection in the love of his enemies:

> *"Father, forgive them; for they know not what they do."*
> *(Lk 23:34)*

Thus Jesus carried God's love for sinful man to the very heart of evil, to the place where this divine Love had been utterly rejected and crucified. Thus, even in his total abandonment, God, in the person of Jesus, was able to be close to sinners so that he could rescue them from the prison that is sin.

The face of Christ on the Turin Shroud is marked by the signs of this total rejection, the marks of violence and

23

torture, the bloodstains, the bruises, the broken nose… Men have rejected the Son of God; they have rejected God himself! These are the ravaged features of Jesus, the Son of God, who has come into the world to offer us his friendship – a friendship that we have instead despised and rejected.

But the death of Jesus on the Cross has a still deeper meaning. He himself knew that his suffering and Crucifixion were endured entirely for the sake of sinful man. He, the Son of God, had freely subjected himself to a human death in order *to give his life as a ransom for many. (Mk 10:45)*

We are standing here before a mystery that our human minds can barely begin to grasp. Jesus Christ placed himself at the mercy of human sinfulness and evil to an extreme and fatal degree, so that he could liberate, could ransom his people from sin, could redeem us all. At the Last Supper with his Twelve Apostles he gave clear expression to this fact:

> *Now as they were eating, Jesus took bread, and blessed and broke it, and gave it to the disciples and said, "Take, eat; this is my body."*
>
> *And he took a cup, and when he had given thanks he gave it to them, saying, "Drink of it, all of you; for this is my blood of the covenant, which is poured out for many for the forgiveness of sins."*
> *(Mt 26:26-28)*

Thus, on the Cross, Jesus offered up his life for the forgiveness of sins and for the redemption of mankind.

24

With absolute trust he placed his fate into the hands of his Heavenly Father:

> *"Father, into thy hands I commit my spirit!"*
> *And having said this he breathed his last.*
> *(Lk 23:46)*

And his trust is not misplaced. His Heavenly Father does not leave him in death but awakens him to new and eternal life. Hence his Resurrection gives to us mortal creatures the hope that we too will one day rise again to new life.

This can perhaps be better understood if we consider the idea of redemption, of atonement – of offering oneself in place of another. All men have something in common; all of us are sinners, from the first moment of human history and without exception. For Adam, the "first man" – and who thus stands as a symbol for all humanity – was the first man to sin and thereby became subject to death (the effect of his sin – which we therefore call Original Sin). As a result all the people of every age have likewise been subject to death.

Therefore Jesus likewise submitted himself – *voluntarily* – to death (although he was without sin and therefore not subject to death) so that he too might share this fate, in common with all humanity. And so, on behalf of all mankind, Jesus submitted in absolute trust and perfect love to the Heavenly Father – thus atoning by his obedience for the disobedience of Adam. Then, by his Resurrection and in the name of all mankind, Jesus accepted the gift of new and everlasting life from his Heavenly Father, as the *"first-born of the dead" (Rev 1:5)*. In this way Jesus has become the 'new Adam'. He lived and died in perfect trust in God, and therefore God has raised him to new life as the representative of all 'new' men.

25

> *"Therefore, if any one is in Christ, he is a new creation; the old has passed away, behold, the new has come."*
> *(2 Cor 5:17)*

These "new" men are those who are "in Christ", as Saint Paul writes. Being "in Christ" means being utterly united with Christ, in a spirit of profound friendship with Christ:

> *For as in Adam all die, so also in Christ shall all be made alive.*
> *(1 Cor 15:22)*

That is why the Holy Shroud, which bears the features of Christ, has such expressive power and depth as a sign of the Incarnation of God, a sign of the closeness of the Kingdom of God, a sign of love and suffering, death and redemption. It is a sign, too, of resurrection and eternal life and of the enduring closeness and presence of Jesus Christ. In short, the entire Good News of Christians is expressed here, in a human face with an aura of the divine.

It is well worth returning frequently to contemplate this face of Christ. Find a quiet moment to sit down "at His feet" and call to mind the precious words that fell from these lips. Reflect inwardly on the love that shone from these eyes, the loving attentiveness with which they once looked out upon the poor and the sick, the rejected and abandoned; the love which embraced even his enemies. Remain for a while in profound silence before this image, in wordless wonder at the love of God, in silent sorrow at the sinfulness of mankind, in confident hope of your own resurrection and in longing certainty of eternal life in God's presence.

Treasured in the heart

Reflect also on the Mother of Jesus, on Mary. The evangelist St Luke, in his account of the birth of Jesus in Bethlehem, describes Our Lady:

> *"But Mary kept all these things, pondering*
> *them in her heart."*
> *(Lk 2: 19)*

Martin Luther translated at this point: "but Mary... turning them over in her heart." Try doing the very same thing yourself. Seek out words in the Sacred Scriptures that appeal to you. But also look out for those words that challenge you, that question you, and perhaps even provoke you. Take them into your heart and ponder them, "turn them over", treasure them in your heart. Carry them everywhere with you.

Chewing and digesting

Maybe you could learn some passages of Scripture by heart. Repeat them to yourself quietly. The early Christian monks sometimes spoke of 'chewing' on the words of the Gospels. Perhaps you have noticed what happens when chewing on wholemeal or granary bread: at first it tastes slightly bitter; but the longer you chew, the more this coarse food turns into sweet tasting bread. You can experience something similar with some, initially bitter-tasting, words of Sacred Scripture. 'Chew' on them, and after a while perhaps they will be transformed into 'sweet food'.

Joy, Light, Sorrow, Glory

There is one particular, very ancient prayer that is based entirely on this principle of meditative 'chewing over'. It is called the Rosary. In it the major events in the life of Jesus are taken into our prayer and thus internalised. This is an ancient and widely proven way of getting to grips with the life of Jesus, of meditating on the life of Jesus, of 'contemplating the face of Christ'. The images that arise from this must spring from within you, must be kept before your own 'spiritual eyes' and dwelt on in your own heart. In this way the words of Scripture are slowly transformed into spiritual 'nourishment' for you.

From words to deeds

Jesus at one point speaks of the will of God as food:

> *"My food is to do the will of him who sent me."*
> *(Jn 4:34)*

At the same time he makes the important point that the words of Scripture are not merely there to be 'consumed', they also call on us to take action. The words of Scripture must be translated into practical deeds. It is not a matter of theory but of practice – our friendship with God must prove itself in everyday life too, in our dealings with our fellow men and women.

Ponder and apply

So try out some of these Gospel words in your daily life. Be brave, experiment! And be creative; make your own experiments with the Word of God.

> *"Since God has destined us to be transformed into the image of his Son, our most important duty is to re-live the life of Christ."*
> *(Father Werenfried van Straaten, founder of Aid to the Church in Need)*

Again, try to imitate Mary, the Mother of God. Treasure in your heart everything that happens to you, all that you personally experience in connection with this Word of God, and ponder upon it.

Here is a tip: you can 'treasure' such experiences with God more easily if from time to time you write them down. Many people keep a regular diary of their friendship with God.

> *"Our influence is not very great. But we can at least ensure that two people follow God's call, that in two people the image of Christ is made visible, that two weak human beings endeavour to be of good will – you and I!"*
> *(Father Werenfried van Straaten)*

"Where two or three gather..."

One final word about reading the Bible: there is a particular promise made by Jesus that applies equally to reading the Holy Scriptures together with other Christians:

Where two or three are gathered in my name,
there am I in the midst of them.
(Mt 18:20)

In a small group of the friends of God, you will find that Jesus Christ can sometimes work in a special way. For he is "in the midst of them" and gives to each of you the gift of his Holy Spirit so that you can understand the Word of God better.

Finding time for God

Just as every friendship among ordinary human beings requires that we spend some time together, so too our friendship with God takes time. If you are truly serious about your friendship with God, then, in just the same way, you should quickly form the good habit of setting aside a more or less regular time to spend with Jesus Christ too. This time that we devote to such conversation with God is what we call prayer. There is a whole range of different ways in which we can spend it.

Basic attitudes to prayer

"And when you pray, you must not be like the hypocrites; for they love to stand and pray in the synagogues and at the street corners, that they may be seen by men. Truly, I say to you, they have received their reward. But when you pray, go into your room and shut the door and pray to your Father who is in secret; and your Father who sees in secret will reward you.

*And in praying do not heap up empty phrases
as the Gentiles do; for they think that they will
be heard for their many words. Do not be like
them, for your Father knows what you need
before you ask him.*

Pray then like this:

*Our Father who art in heaven, Hallowed be
thy name.*

*Thy kingdom come. Thy will be done, on earth
as it is in heaven.*

*Give us this day our daily bread; and forgive
us our debts, as we also have forgiven our
debtors; and lead us not into temptation, but
deliver us from evil."*
(Mt 6:5-13)

Jesus makes it clear to us that prayer is first and foremost something very personal. Individual prayer is not something to be done in public and should above all never be done with any kind of ulterior motive or calculation ("what others might think"). It is an encounter with God, and therefore it should take place in silence and in secret. And so, "go into your room and shut the door". Equally, it is not the number of words that matters, but that your prayer should come from the depths of your heart. Let your prayer be simple and straightforward. Be natural; talk to God just as you would to a good friend.

Sometimes prayer requires a lot of time in order to become truly profound. We know that Jesus frequently withdrew to a solitary place in order to pray, and that he sometimes spent a long time in prayer:

But so much the more the report went abroad
concerning him; and great multitudes
gathered to hear and to be healed of their
infirmities. But he withdrew to the wilderness
and prayed.
(Lk 5:15-16)

Jesus spoke to many people and healed countless of the sick; and yet he never neglected prayer, for this was always of central importance to him.

Prayer requires silence

Silence is a vital precondition for good prayer, as Psalm 131 makes clear. It is a very short psalm of just three verses:

O Lord, my heart is not lifted up, my eyes are
not raised too high; I do not occupy myself
with things too great and too marvellous for
me.

But I have calmed and quieted my soul, like a
child quieted at its mother's breast; like a
child that is quieted is my soul.

O Israel, hope in the Lord from this time forth
and for evermore.
(Psalm 131)

This psalm calls us to an attitude of simplicity and modesty, but also of honesty and sincerity. So be honest with yourself – and also with God.

Hope in the Lord

And then be still. Come to rest. Feel the peace within you becoming ever deeper. And then pray: "Israel, hope in the Lord". If you wish, you can substitute your own name for the name "Israel" (a real person's name). Repeat this phrase for as long as you feel that it is doing good. "Hope in the Lord" means: just wait for God. Look to him for everything. Direct all your yearning towards God, the Lord, your Creator. And do so "from this time forth and for evermore". Make this inner attitude of waiting, hoping and longing into the underlying attitude of your life. Nurture this longing for God. Fill it more and more with meaning. But make yourself ever more familiar with the God of your longing. And then let this longing shine forth in your life and penetrate your entire life through and through – every area of your life. Let your entire life become a mirror of your longing for God.

The Lord's Prayer

In the Jewish and Christian tradition there are many formal prayers. The Lord's Prayer or 'Our Father' is the prayer which Jesus himself gave to his disciples. It contains seven petitions. In the sacred writings, seven is the number of fullness. Hence, in the Lord's Prayer, we find every essential and crucial thing that we can bring before God. It starts by addressing God directly, as our Heavenly Father. God is not distant or inaccessible, a remote being looking down indifferently upon the fate of humanity, upon our sufferings and our need. No, God is close to us, closer even than our own natural father! Christ himself has taught us to address God as 'Father'.

At the same time, *because you are sons, God has sent the Spirit of his Son into our hearts, crying, "Abba! Father!" (Gal 4: 6)*

Following Christ's example, and in the power of the Holy Spirit, we are permitted, in the first three petitions of the Our Father, to request that God's Glory may be made manifest in all its entire splendour – that God's Name may be acknowledged, revered and loved by all mankind and all his creatures, that his Kingdom, the Kingdom of Love, may spread out and come down to us, and that God's Will may prevail everywhere and be done by all, ourselves included. Thus, the first three petitions are all about God – about his Name, his Kingdom, his Will.

The following four petitions are about us human beings. We dare to request that everything we need for life may be granted us by God's hand, above all the "daily bread" – that is to say, the daily nourishment, which by extension also includes the Heavenly Bread of the Eucharist and the Word of God that nourishes us spiritually.

Even in all our human imperfection, weakness and sinfulness, we dare to stand before God and ask the Father of Mercy for the forgiveness of our sins. However, this request presupposes that we too must be willing to forgive others who have offended us.

Finally, in the last two petitions, we call upon God our Father to help us resist the temptation towards evil and to protect us from the workings of the "evil one", that is to say, of Satan, the devil.

The Our Father is the most precious prayer that we Christians possess. No prayer is more profound than this one. The Holy Spirit himself has shaped it. Make this prayer your own. Strive to penetrate its depth and meaning ever more deeply. Pray it often and constantly meditate upon it.

> *"So often I have seen with my own eyes how true the Gospel is. God has never let me down but has always helped me. He always gave me what I asked of him. It is from this that my boundless trust in God has sprung. It has become my second, indeed my true, nature."*
> *(Father Werenfried van Straaten)*

Together before God

The Our Father at the same time makes clear that we can, and should, also stand together before God and pray to him. Those who are united with God should also be united among themselves. This fact is given expression in every liturgical celebration of the Church, and above all in the celebration of the Eucharist. The liturgical Prayer of the Church is also expressed in the Liturgy of the Hours, or Divine Office, which countless Christians today join in – whether they are priests, religious or laity. With hymns, psalms and intercessions this prayer penetrates and hallows with the praise of God the various different hours of the day and the night and the various different times and seasons of the Church's year.

Both the aspects described above are important and necessary – personal prayer, in silence and in private, and prayer in community. See if you can find other people in your immediate circle, especially in your own family, to join you in this communal prayer. There is a special blessing attached to saying this prayer with one's spouse, one's children, as a united family community.

Try to live your friendship with God not as a solitary individual, but instead in the company of other like-minded people. Practise prayer in common. Here too you should strive for a regular pattern of prayer. Perhaps there are people in your neighbourhood who are in need of your prayers. Maybe there are sick people, or the elderly and bedridden, who would be delighted if someone were to pray with them or for them, beside their sickbed. Many formal prayers are suitable for such occasions, such as the Lord's Prayer or the Rosary.

Complete openness to God

God could only become Man in Jesus Christ because there was a woman who assented wholeheartedly to this plan of God and was ready to commit her whole life to it. She was Mary, the Mother of Jesus. In a unique and perfect way she was open to God and his action. In her there was not the slightest opposition to God's will:

> *And Mary said, "Behold, I am the handmaid of the Lord; let it be to me according to your word."*
> *(Lk 1:38)*

Mary understood, and was ready to give herself utterly and completely as the servant of God. Her entire life was one of total submission to the will of God. Hence Mary, the Mother of God, is for us Christians the great model of Faith. We should all seek to follow her example. Her profound unity with God is a perfect pattern for your own life.

The Hail Mary

Mary was capable of this perfect self-giving of her life only because God himself had made her capable of it. This special help from God is what we call grace. Mary received this grace from God in abundance. In perfect freedom, Mary welcomed this grace from God and so allowed it to bear fruit.

It was the Holy Spirit, the creating Spirit who so formed and shaped Mary that she was capable of giving an unconditional and unreserved 'yes' to the plan of God. Through the grace of God she was capable of giving her life entirely to God, so that His will might be done. And so the Holy Spirit was able to prepare the womb of the Virgin Mary and bring about the conception – the Incarnation – of Jesus. In thanksgiving and praise to God for this great gift of grace, through which the Incarnation of God and our own redemption were made possible, Christians have from the earliest times prayed a particular prayer, namely the *Ave Maria*, or Hail Mary:

> *Hail, Mary, full of grace; the Lord is with thee.*
> *Blessed art thou among women, and blessed is*
> *the fruit of thy womb, Jesus.*
>
> *Holy Mary, Mother of God, pray for us sinners*
> *now and at the hour of our death. Amen.*

In saying this prayer you can reflect again and again on the great deeds that are possible in our world when the grace of God comes together with our free and willing cooperation with his will. Pray to God that he may likewise grant you his grace to do his will in this world.

> *"Grant, Mother, when we have passed through*
> *the dark Gate of death and stand before the*

judgment seat of your Son, that we may find
you there, with smiling eyes, and be permitted
to say calmly: Hail, Mother."
(Father Werenfried van Straaten)

The Angelus

There is another ancient prayer, based around the Hail
Mary, which still further unfolds the mystery of God's
Incarnation. It is called the *Angelus*.

> *The Angel of the Lord declared unto Mary,*
> *and she conceived by the Holy Spirit.*
>
> *Hail, Mary, ...etc.*
>
> *Behold the handmaid of the Lord;*
> *be it done unto me according to thy Word.*
>
> *Hail, Mary, ...etc.*
>
> *And the Word became flesh,*
> *and dwelt among us.*
>
> *Hail, Mary, ...etc.*
>
> *Pray for us, O Holy Mother of God,*
> *that we may be made worthy of the promises of*
> *Christ.*
>
> *(Let us pray)*
>
> *Pour forth, we beseech Thee, O Lord, thy*
> *grace into our hearts, that we, to whom the*
> *Incarnation of Christ thy Son was made known*
> *by the message of an angel, may by his*

*Passion and Cross be brought to the glory of
his Resurrection.*

Through Christ Our Lord. Amen.

In the middle of this prayer there is a verse from the Gospel of St John, from the Prologue, right at the beginning of this book. It is a solemn hymn in praise of the "Word" of God. By the "Word" Saint John means Jesus Christ, the Son of God:

> *In the beginning was the Word, and the Word
> was with God, and the Word was God.
> (Jn 1:1)*

It is essential to God's innermost nature that he longs to communicate with us. That is why he created the world and created man within it. God willed to emerge from his hidden-ness and reveal himself to man.

This desire of God existed from the very beginning; hence from the very beginning there was this "Word", the longing of God to communicate himself:

> *All things were made through him, and without
> him was not anything made that was made.
> (Jn 1:3)*

And so it was that through the "Word" the whole of creation – heaven, and earth – came into being. When the time had come *(cf Gal 4:4)*, the "Word" entered the world:

> *And the Word became flesh and dwelt among
> us, full of grace and truth; we have beheld his
> glory, glory as of the only Son from the
> Father.
> (Jn 1:14)*

God could only become Man because there was a woman, Mary, who was open and ready to receive God and his longing to communicate himself.

God sends out his messengers – angels, prophets, and apostles – who bring us news of God; messengers who communicate to us something about the nature of God and about his intentions towards his creation and especially towards mankind.

God sent his Son, Jesus Christ, into this world in order to proclaim to us the Good News of our Redemption, the Good News of the Kingdom of God, the *Gospel* or *Evangelion* (both words mean "good news").

The Holy Spirit helps us to welcome all these messages, to perceive and to understand them.

In the case of Mary, the Mother of God, the Word that came from God was able to operate so effectively that he became Flesh in her virginal womb – the Word that was with God, the Word that *was* God himself, became Man "and dwelt among us", as we have just read in St John's Gospel, above (*Jn 1:14*).

God likewise sends us his Holy Spirit; God also sends us his grace. Provided we are willing to unite ourselves in spirit with the intentions of God, then God's will can become reality in our life and our world too. Then God's will, his Word, can likewise become "flesh" – in other words become reality – in our lives too.

> *"Few people suspect what God could make of them if only they would surrender themselves entirely to him."*
> (Saint Ignatius of Loyola)

Divine interruptions in the midst of everyday life

Following an ancient tradition, the Angelus is usually recited three times a day – in the morning, at noon and in the evening, and wherever possible in community. Thanks to this brief interruption in the midst of the routine of everyday life, you can come back again and again and reflect anew upon what really matters, namely what God plans to achieve with you today, for the welfare of mankind – here and now in your immediate environment. Try to reflect briefly on this at the beginning of your daily work, in the midst of your working day and again at the end of the day as you look back upon it.

In doing so we call upon Mary, the Mother of God, to intercede for us so that "we may be made worthy of the promises of Christ". Through his great act of redemption Jesus Christ has restored us to the dignity of the children of God. We must try to ensure that this dignity shines forth more and more in our daily life.

And we should likewise ask God to fill our hearts with his grace – which means nothing less than to send us his Holy Spirit in fullness, so that we may draw life, as spirit-filled and God-loving souls, from the mystery of the Incarnation of God.

> *"God never refuses his Church the graces she needs."*
> *(Father Werenfried van Straaten)*

Talking as though to a friend

If you interweave your prayer with your daily life in this way, then you can bring your entire life into your prayer, with all its highs and lows, with all its joys and sorrows.

St Teresa of Avila found in her prayer that it is possible to share a great intimacy and confidence with Jesus Christ in prayer:

> *"One can speak to him as to a dear friend,*
> *even though he still remains the Lord."*
> *(Saint Teresa of Avila)*

She was a saint who responded to the invitation of Jesus:

> *"Come to me, all who labour and are heavy laden, and I will give you rest. Take my yoke upon you, and learn from me; for I am gentle and lowly in heart, and you will find rest for your souls. For my yoke is easy, and my burden is light."*
> *(Mt 11:28-30)*

With God you are in safe hands, along with everything that goes to make up your daily life. Talk to Jesus about your life. Talk to him about everything that is on your mind and in your heart.

Daily life as prayer

Prayer is about much more than formal prayers at set times. Every activity that includes God, every time we think about him, all spiritual reading – this is prayer. We should consciously organise such times as times of prayer, with a short prayer at the beginning and at the end – even if it is no more than the Sign of the Cross.

All time devoted to God is prayer. This also includes the times when we are serving God through our work, or through any action done in the service of our fellow men. Doing everything out of love for God and for our fellow men is indeed prayer in its widest sense; it is time spent for God's intentions; and it is time devoted to God:

> *To God be the glory in all that I do.*
> *In work and in leisure,*
> *His will may I treasure,*
> *and praise and honour him too.*
> *My body, my soul, the life that I live,*
> *to God and God only I give,*
> *offering all, Lord Jesus, through you.*
> *(Paraphrased from the German Gotteslob)*

Seeking and finding God in all things

Strive to find God in everything that happens to you. For Saint Ignatius Loyola this was a vital principle of his whole life – to seek and find God in all things, in every duty, in every joy and every sorrow. So entrust yourself to God. Invite him into your life. Offer him your life, just as it is, with all that is beautiful and successful, but at the same time with all your failures and wants, your faults and your sins.

Seek God in everything! And you will find him in quite unexpected ways. Sometimes his presence will be almost tangible, so that you can practically reach out and touch him; at other times you will experience his mysterious

43

hidden-ness and have to endure – and perhaps also suffer – in consequence.

Constant prayer

> *Pray constantly*
> *(1 Thess 5:17)*

There is no conflict between living an active life in the midst of this world and having a profound prayer life (a life of contemplation, to use an ancient Christian term). The two are not mutually exclusive. On the contrary, for the person who would be close to God, a balanced relationship between private personal prayer in silence, communal prayer with others, and prayer in the form of active service for love of God is vital. You should avoid a one-sided approach.

Listening for God 'knocking at the door'

Christians believe that God desires to be close to us, his children, that he seeks our company – but in a mysterious way that is not always easy to perceive or to recognise at first glance:

> *"Behold, I stand at the door and knock; if any*
> *one hears my voice and opens the door, I will*
> *come in to him and eat with him, and he with*
> *me."*
> *(Rev 3:20)*

Often it is through such a gentle 'knocking on the door' that God makes his presence known in our lives. It is a knocking so gentle, however, that it is easily missed if we are not very attentive. You should seek to develop a sensitive hearing, a sense of delicate attentiveness, so that you can discern the signs of God's presence in your life.

The prayer of loving attentiveness

Take a moment, perhaps one evening, and look back on your life, on what has happened that day or in the last few days; look back on your work, on your encounters with other people, within your family, in school or in the workplace, among your circle of friends and acquaintances. Look back again at the good things of the day. What did you do well? What worked out well? Dwell for a moment on this good feeling, and then think of God, your Creator. Perhaps you need say no more than a brief word, like 'thank you'.

Now look back on the other events of the day, or the last few days – on those events that evoke less happy feelings. Where did you fail? Where did you – in retrospect – act wrongly? Why? What happened to disturb or upset you? Where did things not go as you wished? Where did bad things happen to you? Dwell likewise for a moment on these rather less pleasant, and quite possibly unhappy, feelings and then unite them with a short prayer to God your Creator. Once again, you need say no more than a word or two, such as 'Forgive me' or 'Help me'.

Alternatively, you might find it easier to begin this 'prayer of loving attentiveness' (we can also call it an 'examination of conscience') with some words such as those of Psalm 139:

> *O Lord, you search me and you know me, you know my resting and my rising, you discern my*

purpose from afar. You mark when I walk or lie down. All my ways lie open to you.

Before ever a word is on my tongue you know it, O Lord, through and through... If I take the wings of the dawn and dwell at the sea's furthest end, even there your hand would lead me, your right hand would hold me fast...

For it was you who created my being, knit me together in my mother's womb. I thank you for the wonder of my being, for the wonders of all your creation...

O search me God, and know my heart. O test me and know my thoughts. See that I follow not the wrong path and lead me in the path of life eternal.
(Taken from Psalm 139)

The joy and suffering in the world

In your daily life you will meet many other people. On television, radio and in the newspapers you learn much about what is happening in the world. Take all these things into your prayer. Give praise and thanks to God for all the good things in the world, and implore his help for those who are in need. Name names and make specific requests:

"Jesus teaches us expressly that we get what we ask for. He teaches us, in realistic images, that we should not be faint-hearted but that we must persevere and insist, that we must allow God no peace, that we must hammer on his door until deep into the night and pester him

to such an extent that he – simply in order to
be rid of us – can think of no other answer
than to give us what we ask."
(Father Werenfried van Straaten)

Ask the Holy Spirit to inspire you, so that you too can help people around you in their material and spiritual needs. Practise this loving attentiveness towards your fellow men. This too is part of your training in spiritual awareness.

The vine and the branches

Jesus himself gives us the image of the vine and the branches:

> *"I am the true vine, and my Father is the*
> *vinedresser. Every branch of mine that bears*
> *no fruit, he takes away, and every branch that*
> *does bear fruit he prunes, that it may bear*
> *more fruit. You are already made clean by the*
> *word which I have spoken to you. Abide in me,*
> *and I in you. As the branch cannot bear fruit*
> *by itself, unless it abides in the vine, neither*
> *can you, unless you abide in me.*
>
> *I am the vine, you are the branches. He who*
> *abides in me, and I in him, he it is that bears*
> *much fruit, for apart from me you can do*
> *nothing."*
> *(Jn 15: 1-5)*

Picture your own life as a vine, with many branches. There are some branches in your life which bear fruit, some areas of your life and your behaviour, your relationships, etc. in which your life is going well – going well in God's

47

sight too. And God, your Creator, wishes to prune these branches of your life so that they can flourish still more strongly and bear yet more fruit.

Then there are other branches in your life which bear no fruit, which produce only 'dry twigs' or 'rotten fruit'. It is better for these 'unfruitful branches' to be cut right out. In this way the other, good branches, will grow all the better and be able to bear still more fruit. Notice too, in this imagery of Jesus, how important it is for your life to remain joined to Christ – in other words to the rootstock itself. Only branches such as these, that are connected by a living bond to the rootstock, and which are nourished by the living sap from the roots, can bear fruit. So it is with your life too. Only in close and living union with Jesus can you make your life a fruitful one.

> *"Christ refuses to belong to the past. He wants to be more than a vague figure from a parable of two thousand years ago. He wishes to be our contemporary; he wants to live on in his Church. What he once did in his own person he now wishes to repeat until the end of time in all those who bear his name."*
> *(Father Werenfried van Straaten)*

God, your Creator, wants to work together with you and make something beautiful of your life. Just as the vine grower tends and cares for his vineyard, so too God wants to act in your life, so that it becomes 'fruitful'. If you refuse this loving care of God, then your life will bear only 'bitter fruit'. It is precisely this that lies at the core of human sin – the refusal of the creative love of God! If, however, you let God act in you, then your life will bear good fruit in abundance. During your time of contemplation, of examination of conscience, you are scrutinising your life together with God, your Creator.

Together you will establish where it is growing and blossoming and flourishing and bearing fruit, and also where things are withering, barren, misshapen and distorted.

> For we are his workmanship, created in Christ Jesus for good works, which God prepared beforehand, that we should walk in them.
> (Eph 2:10)

Test all things – hold fast to the good

The prayer of loving attentiveness is the time and place of testing, the proving-ground of which Saint Paul speaks:

> Test everything; hold fast what is good, abstain from every form of evil.
> (1 Thess 5:21-22)

Learn to distinguish the good from the bad, the genuine from the fake, the true from the false, the valuable from the worthless. Place yourself – quite consciously and with great determination – on the side of good, on the side of God! Learn to love God and to reject all that is evil. Don't shrink from the effort of tackling all your familiar, but bad, habits and casting them off. Don't try to deceive yourself – or God – but rather strive to be honest and truthful. Endeavour in time to overcome the bad things in your own life; step out of the kingdom of shadow, of darkness and distortion and step forward with courage towards a life in the Light:

> For once you were darkness, but now you are light in the Lord; walk as children of light (for the fruit of light is found in all that is good and

*right and true), and try to learn what is
pleasing to the Lord.*

*Take no part in the unfruitful works of
darkness, but instead expose them.*
(Eph 5:8-11)

There is a great deal of shadow and darkness in today's
world – for example in the media and the entertainment
industry. Be on your guard in this area in particular. Be
discerning in your choice of films, books, and magazines.
Remember to test all things and choose 'what is pleasing
to the Lord'. Try to live consciously as a child of God – in
that way you will never be living a life that is morally
unsound.

Discernment of spirits

You should also try to distinguish between the various
different impulses within you and to identify their origin.
For instance, where was God's Holy Spirit at work in your
life? Where are the traces of this Spirit to be found? The
fruits of the Spirit include especially such qualities as love,
joy, peace, patience, kindness, goodness, gentleness and
self-control (see *Gal 5:22-23*).

On the other hand, where was your own will at work? Was
it in conformity with the will of God – did you seek to
make God's will your own? Or was your own will wilful –
in other words, contrary to the will of God? If so then the
possible consequences might well have included impurity,
licentiousness, idolatry, sorcery, enmity, strife, jealousy,
anger, selfishness, dissension, party spirit, envy,
drunkenness and the like (see *Gal 5:19-22*).

Again, were there perhaps traces of the 'evil spirit' in your life? Signs of the devil, perhaps – the *diabolos* (a Greek word, roughly meaning 'disorderer', 'sower of confusion'), who seeks to destroy and undermine God's good order? The devil, or Satan (the 'enemy'), is indeed the enemy of God and the enemy of man. His workings in our world are subtle and sometimes hard to detect, but we must be always on our guard and ready for his attacks.

Try to reinforce the good inclinations in your life and to check and overcome the bad ones. All three influences – God's good Spirit, our own often wilful spirit and the spirit of the evil one – are simultaneously at work in our world. Christians believe and trust that in the end God's Holy Spirit will prevail.

Closer to God – or further from him?

Another method of discernment is to ask yourself whether particular actions and attitudes tend to bring you closer to God or rather draw you away from him. Do they strengthen your faith in God, your hope in Salvation and eternal Life, your love for God and for your fellow men? Do they strengthen what we call the three 'Theological Virtues' – that is, Faith, Hope and Love (or Charity) or do they weaken them?

A particular vocation for you alone?

In this intensive time of prayer you will perhaps also discover that God has quite specific plans for you personally, that he wishes to entrust to you certain particular duties, whether large or small, that you alone can fulfil. Perhaps he even has a specific life mission for

51

you! Reflect on these things too when you pray. And talk about them to people you trust, especially with a priest, if possible.

Living with the Church

The prayer of loving attentiveness and the discernment of spirits will come easier to you the more familiar you are with the Christian Faith. The Church which Jesus Christ founded has guarded and treasured his Good News for two thousand years. During this long period she has, with the help of the Holy Spirit, penetrated ever more deeply into the Gospel of Jesus Christ and learnt to understand it better. Hence the Church can give you useful help in living a life that is fruitful in the eyes of God. Make use of the Church's help; make use also of the opportunity to talk to a priest. Make use, too, of the written aids which the Church provides. For example, there are a range of different catechisms, both for young people and for adults. They set out and explain the Christian and Catholic Faith. If you read such a catechism regularly, even just for half an hour every Sunday, you will learn to understand God better and better, and your friendship with him will grow deeper.

There are also many good books, written by saints and spiritual writers, that can help you further. Again, ask a priest; he will certainly be able to recommend you something that is suited to you in your particular situation.

Time out in the wilderness

There is a still more intensive form of spiritual recollection which consists of taking time out from everyday life. It will enable you to deepen your friendship with God if, occasionally – for example every few months, or perhaps even once a month – you withdraw for a day with the Sacred Scriptures or another good religious book, or even with your own personal diary, to a lonely place, in order to be alone with God. This is similar to the practice of the early Christian monks, who withdrew into the desert in order to be alone with God. Another, perhaps easier, way would be to set aside half an hour – or more – each Sunday for this. After all, Sunday is the day of the Lord!

Praise and complaint – the Psalms

Jesus was a man for whom prayer was of vital importance. We know that he had absorbed so many of the psalms that he knew them by heart.

The collection of the psalms was the prayer book of the people of Israel. They arose over the course of centuries and include prayers for every situation in life. With great openness, the psalms bring every situation and every emotion of man before God – rejoicing, joy, gratitude, wonder at creation and the great deeds of God, but at the same time also need and suffering, fervent pleading, bitter complaint addressed to God, incomprehension at the injustice of the world and the seeming absence of God.

The Psalms are an inexhaustible treasury for inspiring your own prayer. Seek out those particular psalms, or psalm verses, that appeal to you or that suit your own particular situation at the time. Write them down on a sheet of paper and place them in your little prayer corner, or carry them with you, in your wallet or handbag. Or maybe you can learn them by heart, so that you can carry them with you everywhere, in your heart. Bring these verses into your everyday life and see what they can do for you. Do things seem better when you pray them? Do they make you feel different? Do they bring you closer to God? Try it, and see what happens.

Words for every situation in life

Here are some examples of verses from the Psalms that might help you in your own personal prayer:

Bless the Lord, O my soul! O Lord my God, thou art very great! Thou art clothed with honour and majesty.
(Ps 104:1)

I will extol thee, my God and King, and bless thy name for ever and ever.
(Ps 145:1)

The Lord is my light and my salvation; whom shall I fear? The Lord is the stronghold of my life; of whom shall I be afraid?
(Ps 27:1)

As a hart longs for flowing streams, so longs my soul for thee, O God.

My soul thirsts for God, for the living God. When shall I come and behold the face of God?
(Ps 42:1-2)

O God, thou art my God, I seek thee, my soul thirsts for thee; my flesh faints for thee, as in a dry and weary land where no water is.
(Ps 63:1)

But I am poor and needy; hasten to me, O
God! Thou art my help and my deliverer; O
Lord, do not tarry!
(Ps 70:5)

Save me, O God! For the waters have come up
to my neck.
(Ps 69:1)

In thee, O Lord, do I take refuge; let me never
be put to shame!
(Ps 71:1)

Keep me as the apple of the eye; hide me in the
shadow of thy wings,
(Ps 17:8)

Thou hast turned for me my mourning into
dancing; thou hast loosed my sackcloth and
girded me with gladness, that my soul may
praise thee and not be silent. O Lord my God,
I will give thanks to thee for ever.
(Ps 30:12-13)

Prayer as poetry – Poets of prayer

They were poets, the men who wrote these prayers. And
they were close friends of God as well. They lived with
God, searched for God and wrestled with God. Do you
sense the intensity, the depth of these psalms?

Perhaps you will even discover a poetic vein in yourself.
Why not try composing your own Psalm verses? Be
creative, be inventive. In this way you are responding to
God, who himself is the greatest and most creative of

artists. You can be sure that this will enrich your prayer life.

Many of the Psalm verses are ideally suited as short 'ejaculatory prayers' – short, spontaneous, heartfelt prayers, uttered from time to time during the day, through which you can renew your sense of closeness to God. Make use of such impulsive prayers frequently, to place yourself consciously in the abiding presence of God.

Staying close to God – in the power of the Holy Spirit

By living close to God in this way, we can discover within ourselves a power through which our relationship with him is strengthened and deepened. This power does not come from us but from God. For it is the Holy Spirit who initiates, shapes and strengthens our bond with God:

> *Likewise the Spirit helps us in our weakness;*
> *for we do not know how to pray as we ought,*
> *but the Spirit himself intercedes for us with*
> *sighs too deep for words.*
> *(Rom 8:26)*

Those who are close to God in this way are therefore 'spiritual' people – in other words people who in their thinking, feeling and actions are moved and guided by the Spirit of God, by the Holy Spirit. Baptised Christians have, by virtue of their baptism (sealed by the sacrament of Confirmation), established contact with the Holy Spirit. Everything in the Christian life comes down to making room for the action of the Holy Spirit, opening oneself up to the workings of the Holy Spirit, working in cooperation with the creating Spirit and in this way shaping one's life.

Baptism was the beginning. Now what we have to do is take what was begun in Baptism, develop it in our ongoing lives and bring it to its full 'flourishing'. That is why it is so important to remind ourselves again and again of our own Baptism and to make ourselves consciously and constantly aware of the vocation that was thereby conferred on us to live our life with God. Christians are baptised "in the name of the Father and of the Son and of the Holy Spirit". Every time you make the Sign of the Cross, therefore, you should consciously remind yourself that you have been baptised and destined for a life lived in union with God. This reminder of your Baptism will have added symbolism if you first dip your finger in holy water. Do this, for example, every time you enter or leave a church. Another good and ancient custom is to have a small holy water stoup in your own home, perhaps in your prayer corner. Or at the door to your home – then every time you leave the house you can make the Sign of the Cross with Holy Water and thereby call down God's protection on all your ways and his blessing on all your doings in the world. Another beautiful sign is to take holy water at the beginning and end of the day and, by making the Sign of the Cross, to place your own life and that of your family and all your nearest and dearest under the blessing and protection of Almighty God.

Planning your day – with God

By now you have encountered many of the elements that should characterise your friendship with God. Keep this friendship alive and let it grow deeper. You will find that this growing never comes to an end your whole life long.

Try and see if it helps you to establish your life with God on the basis of regular prayer times. Draw up a small timetable with set times for silence, Scripture reading and prayer. Experiment with this timetable and change it until it suits you personally. A certain amount of regularity will undoubtedly improve your friendship with God!

Never forget, God is your Creator. He has given you life. Never cease to tell him how grateful you are to him for this.

Consciously welcome each morning as coming from God's hands, with a short greeting to your Creator as an expression of thanks. In your daily work you can share in the shaping of the world. God has entrusted his Creation into our hands. Do everything in the conscious awareness that you have been entrusted by God to shape this creation for the good of all humanity.

Each evening, place the day that is past, with everything in it, with all its work, its burdens and its joys back in God's hands, returning them with love to your Creator. In the prayer of loving attentiveness you can look back with God upon your life.

It goes without saying that the food you eat is what keeps you alive. But ultimately all this food likewise comes from the hand of your Creator, who made the plants and the animals. Hence it is an honourable custom to give thanks to your Creator in a few brief words before every meal. Similarly, after eating, we ask his blessing on ourselves and all our doings as we return to our daily duties. Every moment we stop to eat is likewise a brief interruption in the work of the day. Make use of this moment consciously, to converse briefly with your Creator. In doing so you can remember the words of Jesus:

Man shall not live by bread alone, but by every
word that proceeds from the mouth of God.
(Mt 4:4)

We often eat together in common – in the family, with friends, in the workplace. Where circumstances permit, try to say this prayer of thanksgiving (we call it 'grace', which means 'thanksgiving') together to your Maker. If not, then pray in silence, with an unobtrusive symbolic gesture (you can always make that simple, yet powerful, gesture –the Sign of the Cross).

Life through the Sacraments – the Eucharist

In the Holy Scriptures we learn everything we need to know about God and his plans for mankind, about the friendship and love he offers us. Above all we find Jesus Christ there, God's Son, our Saviour, Friend and Redeemer.

In prayer we respond to the love of God and engage in conversation with our divine Friend. In the moments of silence and contemplation we listen for the gentle knocking of God on the door and try to discern his will for our own personal life.

In this way, through reading the Scriptures and through prayer, we experience the encounter with God. However, God has devised something else that is intended to lead you into still more profound communion with him. This is the Eucharistic Banquet:

Behold, I stand at the door and knock; if any
one hears my voice and opens the door, I will

*come in to him and eat with him, and he with
me.*
(Rev 3:20)

In the Gospel you will find numerous accounts of how Jesus sat down to eat with the people, with his disciples and friends. He cared particularly about those people who were still far from God, who had strayed from the right path. Jesus was constantly going in search of the 'lost' ones in order to bring them home into the Kingdom of God, into communion with God. For he had come "not to call the righteous, but sinners." (*Mt 9:13*). Some of the Pharisees referred to him as the "friend of tax collectors and sinners" (*Lk 7:34*).

It was people such as these whom Jesus invited to eat with him and so to restore their friendship with God. Having a meal together is a sign of deep friendship and communion. After his Resurrection, Jesus also made use of this sign. The evangelist St Luke tells us of his meeting with the disciples on the way to Emmaus and how the risen Lord shared a meal with them (*Lk 24:13-35*).

But there was one meal that had a quite special significance. This was the last meal that Jesus ate with his disciples, on the eve of his suffering and death:

*And he said to them, "I have earnestly desired
to eat this passover with you before I suffer."*
(Lk 22:15)

In a sense it was indeed a farewell meal. For in this particular moment Christ was creating something entirely new, a totally new form of encounter and communion with God. The gifts of bread and wine, symbols of the good creation of God, were now to become divine Food: "Take; this is my body." (*Mk 14:22*) "This is my blood of the covenant, which is poured out for many." (*Mk 14:24*) "Do this in remembrance of me." (*Lk 22:19*)

Imagine to yourself a very human experience, such as the farewell between two people who love each other. They would like to be together for ever but some duty forces them to part. Their dearest wish would be never to part, but this is not possible for them.

Since human love, however great it may be, meets with limitations, it must be assisted with outward signs, such as a photo bearing words of such ardent devotion that you might think the very paper would burst into flames. This is the most we can do, for our human powers do not extend as far as our wishes.

But the Lord can do what we cannot. Jesus Christ, perfect God and perfect Man, has left us not a sign, but a reality. It is he himself who remains. He will go to the Father and remain among men.

He does not merely give us a gift to keep alive our memory of him, such as a picture which fades and blurs with time, or a photo that yellows with age and seems worthless to those who were not present at the time.

He himself is truly present, under the outward appearance of bread and wine. He is present with his body, his blood, his soul and his divinity.
(St Josemaria Escrivá, founder of Opus Dei)

For almost 2,000 years now, we Christians have been gathering regularly to celebrate the 'Banquet of the Lord' in order to keep alive the memory of Jesus Christ. But there is much more to it than this. For under the outward form of bread and wine, transformed by the power of the Holy Spirit into the Body and Blood of Christ, Jesus Christ is truly present among us in a unique manner. In this banquet we are in the presence of a mystery that exceeds the power of our human understanding. Trusting faith, sincere wonder and adoration are the only appropriate responses:

> *Godhead here in hiding, whom I do adore*
> *Masked by these bare shadows, shape and*
> *nothing more,*
> *See, Lord, at thy service low lies here a heart*
> *Lost, all lost in wonder at the God thou art.*
> *Seeing, touching, tasting are in thee deceived;*
> *How says trusty hearing? That shall be*
> *believed;*
> *What God's Son hath told me, take for truth I*
> *do;*
> *Truth himself speaks truly, or there's nothing*
> *true.*
> *(St Thomas Aquinas, Adoro te Devote,*
> *translated by Gerard Manley Hopkins)*

We are invited to receive this divine food and so to unite ourselves in the most intimate possible manner with Jesus Christ; with God himself. The Eucharistic gifts of bread and wine are the signs of the New Covenant that Christ has made with us.

> *He who eats my flesh and drinks my blood*
> *abides in me, and I in him.*
> *(Jn 6:56)*

62

Here on earth the longing of our soul can find no more perfect fulfilment than in this union with Christ. Through Holy Communion (from the Latin word *communio* meaning communion, or union), through the Eucharistic gifts of bread and wine, your hunger for God is satisfied in an altogether unique manner:

> *O God, thou art my God, I seek thee, my soul*
> *thirsts for thee; my flesh faints for thee, as in a*
> *dry and weary land where no water is.*
> *(Ps 63:1)*

It is Jesus Christ himself who invites us to share in the Eucharist. Hence our willingness to respond to this invitation is a sign of how seriously we mean our friendship with God.

Try to participate regularly in the celebration of the Eucharist. Seek this encounter with Christ every Sunday in Holy Mass. Endeavour to understand the meaning and significance of the celebration of the Mass and its individual elements more and more fully. Perhaps you can even find time and opportunity to attend Holy Mass during the week as well, for it is Christ himself whom we encounter there! Seek him in Holy Mass – and you will indeed find him!

With regard to Holy Communion, please note that it requires a particular interior preparation. Be always conscious of the great gift you are receiving, for it is God himself! Think carefully beforehand as to whether you are inwardly ready to receive God. Or has there perhaps been a serious breach of trust, a grave wounding of your friendship with God, a grave sin? If so, you must first seek reconciliation with God in the Sacrament of Penance. You must first of all heal this breach of friendship before you can allow yourself to come again to the Table of the Lord.

This is a binding law of the Church. By doing so you will come to understand, through your own experience, what the celebration of the Eucharist is ultimately all about – for it concerns the dark mystery of sin and death, and Jesus Christ who overcame and defeated both and who will lead God's creation to its final perfection.

Sin and death have lost their power

In the Eucharist we celebrate our liberation from all that seeks to destroy our life – on the one hand there is the power of the evil one, who seeks to lead our lives astray and cause them to founder completely, and on the other there is the power of death, which can utterly annihilate and extinguish our earthly life.

By offering his life on the Cross, Jesus has liberated mankind from the power of sin, and by his Resurrection he has destroyed death. These two destructive forces – sin and death – no longer have any power over man. Figuratively speaking, they can still loom large in our lives and throw them massively into confusion (remember *diabolos*, the sower of confusion). But of this we can be absolutely certain: by the offering of his life and by his Resurrection, Jesus Christ has finally defeated these destructive powers. Every person who is a true friend of Jesus Christ is on the side of the divine Victor, who guarantees him indestructible, eternal life.

In the Holy Mass we celebrate the memorial of the sacrifice of Christ and, because of our friendship with him, we seek to commit our lives, too, and to offer them for the Kingdom of God by serving our fellow men in a spirit of Christian charity.

In our everyday life we frequently encounter the powers of destruction which distort and disfigure the life of our fellow human beings, crushing or even extinguishing them. Many of these destructive powers have their origin in the natural forces of the earth, others rage in the form of deadly illnesses. However, most of the destructive powers

65

have their origin in the human heart, for they spring from our own sinfulness, the sinfulness of those who refuse or are incapable of establishing peace and justice among their fellow men.

Inspiration and strength to shape the world

The celebration of the Eucharist is the place where Christians can draw strength – the strength of divine grace – to combat the life-threatening powers in our world and overcome them, and to support the life-sustaining tendencies and enable them to prevail. The Mass concludes with the dismissal, the 'sending out' of the faithful back into their everyday life. This is the time to display courage and perseverance in our Faith. Now it is time to do the will of God in all the different dimensions of human society – in the family, the school, the workplace, the local neighbourhood, one's circle of friends, one's parish, in wider society, in politics, culture and science. Not one area of life should remain exempt!

> *"Not every one who says to me, 'Lord, Lord,'*
> *shall enter the kingdom of heaven, but he who*
> *does the will of my Father who is in heaven."*
> *(Mt 7:21)*

It is a good practice to take a verse from the readings or the Gospel at your Sunday Mass, or perhaps a phrase from the sermon, into your daily life for the coming week. Try to reflect upon this verse or phrase from time to time and to put it into practice wherever possible in some concrete action. Ask yourself how well you managed – or didn't, and maybe even make a note of your experience in your diary, for future reference.

*"In the Eucharist we encounter Jesus in the
form of bread and wine; in the suffering and
needy we do so in the form of flesh and
blood."*
(Father Werenfried van Straaten)

Nazareth – daily life divinely lived

Another intriguing exercise is to meditate occasionally on
how Jesus Christ – the Son of God! – might have lived his
daily life in Nazareth. He was the carpenter's son and
before his public life began at the age of around 30 (see *Lk
3:23*) he himself worked for many years as a carpenter
(see *Mk 6:3*). The gospels tell us little about these 'hidden
years' in Nazareth, but Saint Luke records that *Jesus
increased in wisdom and in stature, and in favour with
God and man. (Lk 2:52)*

So how might Jesus have lived his life? Was it the normal
round of working week and Sabbath, of toil and rest? How
did he live with his family, with his parents, with his close
and more distant relatives? And how about his
neighbours? His colleagues in the building trade? What
about the employers, the architects, the timber merchants?

What kind of buildings might he have built? Simple
dwellings in Nazareth? Or did he work on larger building
sites in the bigger towns? Did he work only for Jews or for
Roman employers too? How did he deal with the trials of
daily work, with the hard work, the monotony, with
success and failure, with the need to earn one's daily
bread? How might he have spent his leisure time? Was
there time for companionship and games? Were there
children in his extended family whom he cared for
occasionally? Did he tend to old or sick people? How

might his religious life have been shaped – his prayer, the times of worship, the religious festivals?

Much of what Jesus experienced in Nazareth and elsewhere can be found in his parables. "He increased in wisdom" can be taken to mean that even Jesus himself went through a phase of development! He grew and developed further, not resting on what he had already achieved. And he grew "in favour with God and man".

But what is the significance of this hidden life of God in the everyday life of Nazareth? The son of God – unrecognised among men – as a simple craftsman. God himself has shared the everyday life of ordinary men, and for many years. Does that not give human work a quite particular, divine dignity?

We know a great deal about Jesus, about his views and attitudes, from his public life. But we do not know how he translated all this and lived it beforehand, in his own daily life in Nazareth. It is our task, as Christians and friends of God, to imitate the life of Jesus in Nazareth – in our own particular daily life, in our own Nazareth. We too must strive to give our work a divine dignity, to 'sanctify' both our work and our everyday life – by uniting it all with God. This, too, and indeed this precisely, is what the imitation of Jesus means:

> *"Let the risen Christ rule in you, so that*
> *through his transforming power you may*
> *become new men. Do not seek life among the*
> *dead, among the selfish ones. Act according to*
> *Jesus's own words: 'A new commandment I*
> *give to you, that you love one another.' Then*
> *you will indeed become new men and women,*
> *like Peter, John, the women, the disciples of*

Emmaus. They no longer feared; they bore witness instead, for they had love."
(Father Werenfried van Straaten)

In conversation with Jesus Christ

Hence you should try to bring your daily life into your friendship with Jesus Christ. Talk to him in prayer about your life, your daily cares. Jesus understands our human life, he understands our daily struggles! He will understand all your concerns.

Seek this dialogue with Christ, especially at Holy Mass. If you can't find the time to participate in the celebration of the Eucharist during your working day, then at least take the opportunity, wherever it presents itself, to visit Jesus Christ in a Catholic Church or chapel – to 'drop in on him' in passing, so to speak. In such places you can be especially close to him. For Christ is enduringly present here in the Blessed Sacrament that is preserved in the Tabernacle. A small red light, the 'perpetual light' of the sanctuary lamp, is usually the sign that he is present.

Stay with him for a few minutes; in wordless silence, in quiet adoration, in reverence and love, conversing with him about your own cares and concerns.

Such honouring of the Son of God, Jesus Christ in the Eucharistic Bread, will bring a particular blessing on your friendship with Christ.

Additionally, in many churches, the ancient and venerable custom continues of exposing the Blessed Sacrament, the 'Holiest of Holies' as it is called, in a precious display vessel, known as a *monstrance*, and placing it on the altar for Eucharistic adoration. Try especially to take advantage of such opportunities for prayer before your Eucharistic Lord. You will find it a source of immense graces!

The great refusal

When you do pray in an opened church in front of the Blessed Sacrament, you will find that you are more often than not either quite alone or in the company of just a handful of other silent adorers. Jesus Christ, the Son of God, is really and truly present there, and he waits for us. He offers us his friendship and love. But not all people respond to this. Many remain indifferent, and many even reject God entirely!

If you reflect occasionally about this dark mystery of the refusal of God, you may after a time detect some traces of this same rejection in yourself too – the refusal of the friendship of Jesus. You yourself may have rejected God. Of course, yours is not a fundamental rejection, but nonetheless we do all reject him again and again in little things – and sometimes in considerably bigger things! Jesus has shown himself our truest friend, yet we still reject him at times! His friendship is spurned, his friendship betrayed. How are we to understand this contradictory behaviour?

> *For I do not do the good I want, but the evil I do not want is what I do. Now if I do what I do not want, it is no longer I that do it, but sin which dwells within me. So I find it to be a law that when I want to do right, evil lies close at hand.*
> *(Rom 7:19-21)*

The Church knows all too well about this mysterious weakness of man, about his incapacity to love God. For she knows a great deal about the mystery of evil in the world. The overcoming of this weakness, the overcoming of our sins, is a part of the art of falling in love with God. Indeed, it is the hardest part of all and requires a great deal of patience and practice. Let the Church help you here, for she has 2,000 years of experience of our human frailty.

There are all kinds of ways in which we can neglect our friendship with God, can give him too little of our time and attention, can even injure and damage this friendship. We can even completely lose sight of this friendship and end up feeling utterly indifferent towards God.

Indeed, we can consciously refuse God, can resist all his overtures of friendship and entirely reject him. We can completely deny our God, the Creator of our lives. This is the gravest imaginable breach of friendship – the total rupture of our friendship with him. It leads to the loss of the very source of our lives and so to eternal death – in total separation from the life-giving God. This total refusal of the friendship of God (which in practice is equivalent to enmity with him) can only result from a refusal on our human side. God, who is love itself and full of kindness and mercy, still longs to hold in his arms every one of these enemies who displays even the smallest readiness for conversion, just like the loving father in Our Lord's parable of the Prodigal Son. (*Lk 15: 11-32*)

Turning back to God

Even when we try to follow a path that brings us closer to God, we find again and again that we lose our way and wander from this path. At this point it is absolutely essential not to continue on this false path we have taken, but to turn round and find our way back to the right path. This turning back, or conversion, to God was the central message of Jesus Christ:

> *Jesus came into Galilee, preaching the gospel of God, and saying, "The time is fulfilled, and the kingdom of God is at hand; repent, and believe in the gospel."*
> *(Mk 1:14-15)*

Jesus left us a sacrament especially for this purpose. It is the Sacrament of Reconciliation, or Penance, and it provides us with an effective remedy for overcoming the power of sin and turning back to God.

> *"I fear for a Christianity that seeks to adapt the commandments of God to our human weakness, instead of striving daily, with a repentant heart, to rise again from our sins."*
> *(Father Werenfried van Straaten)*

Life through the sacraments – Confession

In the Sacrament of Penance, all the baggage of sin, everything that weighs down and darkens our friendship with God, is cleared away and swept aside! All your sins, everything that blocks the path between you and God, are wiped away by God himself.

But this is not like an operation conducted under anaesthetic, and while we are unconscious. No indeed, for God takes you seriously. He wants you to be consciously aware of the situation in which you stand. Your friendship with God relies upon a growing awareness of his forgiveness and it is this which enables the relationship to deepen.

You must strive to find out your own weaknesses and faults, shining the bright light of truth on every area of your life. Probe your conscience, and make use of written aids, such as the examinations of conscience that you can find in many everyday prayer books. You might also find the jottings in your spiritual diary helpful here. For it is only in this way that you can come to know yourself as you truly are, to know yourself as a sinner before God.

Try to discern just how deeply you have damaged your friendship with God, the God of your life, by your failings and wrongful actions. You should have feelings of sorrow, a painful sense of your own failure and unfaithfulness:

> *And Peter remembered the saying of Jesus,*
> *"Before the cock crows, you will deny me*
> *three times." And he went out and wept*
> *bitterly.*
> *(Mt 26:75)*

Remember though, this sorrow is a healthy and healing sorrow. Don't try to suppress it. Don't be ashamed of your tears! They are a sign of deep repentance in you, and your genuine sorrow will lead you back into the arms of God.

And then, when you kneel before the priest in the Sacrament of Penance, you will have the courage to declare your failings towards God, speaking openly and unaffectedly. In this sacrament of forgiveness you will find that God's love is far greater than your sins. God loves you, despite your sins, and forgives you everything. Nowhere else can you feel God's love for you more deeply!

Make the most of this opportunity for returning to God. We are all sinners and will remain so for all our lives. That is why conversion to God is an ongoing task. Try to find a priest who is kind and understanding and try to come back to this Sacrament of Reconciliation – or Confession – regularly. Your confessor will help you to find the right pattern. And this sacrament will change your life!

> *Create in me a clean heart, O God, and put a new and right spirit within me. Cast me not away from thy presence, and take not thy holy Spirit from me. Restore to me the joy of thy salvation, and uphold me with a willing spirit. (Ps 51:10-12)*

Seeking God's company – the temptations of the evil one

Anyone who tries to come close to God, who tries earnestly to find him, sooner or later discovers within himself times of inner 'conflict'. At certain moments these can become unusually severe, and then we should ask ourselves if perhaps there is 'somebody' behind it. The Bible speaks clearly of the devil, the *diabolos* (the Greek word means 'sower of confusion'). Jesus himself had a particularly intensive experience of this 'evil spirit' when he spent 40 days in the desert, preparing for the beginning of his public life by devoting himself to prayer and fasting. The disciples of Jesus also had similar experiences. In St Luke's Gospel Jesus says to Simon Peter:

> *"Simon, Simon, behold, Satan demanded to have you, that he might sift you like wheat, but I have prayed for you that your faith may not*

fail; and when you have turned again,
strengthen your brethren."
(Lk 22:31-32)

Thus God knows about the dangers which especially affect those people who strive to deepen their friendship with God. Jesus Christ prayed for his disciples. And he prays for us too, that we may not lose our Faith (yes, God himself is praying for us – what a sign of his loving concern for us!). Those who have come through such difficult times and found their way to a firm Faith should now strive to help their brothers and sisters in their difficulties with the Faith, and seek to support and strengthen them. Simon Peter himself, in the first of his letters that have come down to us, calls for watchfulness against the attacks of Satan:

> *Be sober, be watchful. Your adversary the*
> *devil prowls around like a roaring lion,*
> *seeking some one to devour. Resist him, firm in*
> *your faith, knowing that the same experience*
> *of suffering is required of your brotherhood*
> *throughout the world.*
> *(1 Pet 5:8-9)*

When St Peter describes the devil as a "roaring lion" he is reminding us of the great danger that Satan poses. You should also soberly take account of this danger and practise inner watchfulness. And remember, the closer we try to come to God, the more fiercely this 'wrecker' will try to stop us!

Seeking God – and the silence of God

But it is not only the devil who can be the source of confusion and trials. There are times, as many of the saints have reported, when, despite our most earnest efforts, we no longer feel the immediate presence of God. The prophet Isaiah expresses this experience when he says:

> *Truly, thou art a God who hidest thyself, O*
> *God of Israel, the Saviour.*
> *(Is 45:15)*

Even when we seek God's presence, and indeed sometimes clearly sense it, yet God will always remain a mystery. He is great, and at many times – or indeed most of the time – in a certain sense unapproachable. Many of the saints relate their experience of dark times and trials of faith, and Saint John of the Cross speaks of the "dark night of the soul" in which we can no longer see or feel anything of God. Saint Therese of Lisieux writes:

> *But in the joyful days of Eastertide Jesus*
> *permitted the deepest darkness to penetrate my*
> *soul and the thought of Heaven, otherwise so*
> *sweet to me, became nothing more than an*
> *occasion of struggle and torments… One has*
> *to have gone through this dark tunnel in order*
> *to understand just how dark it is.*

At such times our faith becomes difficult. Did Jesus also know such times of darkness in Faith?

> *My God, my God, why hast thou forsaken me?*
> *(Mk 15:34)*

Perhaps, in meditating on the image on the Turin Shroud, you may also detect some signs of this sense of abandonment by God:

> *And Jesus uttered a loud cry, and breathed his last.*
> *(Mk 15:37)*

For does not this image show us the dead Christ who has "breathed his last"?

But God has not remained silent! The Creator has the last word – always! He spoke the word that awakened Jesus to new life! This is the hope, even in the deepest, most impenetrable darkness; the hope, even in the very moment of death; the hope that remains, for you and me also!

And so we must always entrust our lives, again and again, into the hands of our Creator:

> *Then Jesus, crying with a loud voice, said,*
> *"Father, into thy hands I commit my spirit!"*
> *And having said this he breathed his last.*
> *(Lk 23:46)*

If you find it hard to endure the hidden-ness of God and his mysterious silence (this too is a part of your friendship with God), then speak to a priest about it. But whatever you do, hold fast to your friendship with God!

Small tokens of friendship

Your friendship with God can be strengthened and consolidated by small external signs of friendship. Just as a husband and wife express their union by wearing a wedding ring, so our union with God can be expressed by

77

small but tangible symbols. Many Christians wear a small cross around their neck, blessed by a priest; others perhaps wear a ring that has been specially blessed. Others always carry a blessed Rosary with them, not only as an aid to prayer but as a constant reminder of their personal friendship with God. There are also little medals of various kinds and designs that one can wear round the neck or carry in one's purse or wallet. You might also find it helpful to have a small picture of Christ as a bookmark in your diary.

Such small devotional symbols blessed by a priest are known as *sacramentals* by the Church. They are a source of grace and a way of keeping alive our awareness of God in our everyday lives. This living relationship with God will in turn bring blessings on your life and work. Symbols of this kind will remind you of the constant presence of God and help you, especially in difficult situations or moments of danger, so that you can entrust yourself in every situation to the protection of God.

The Communion of Saints – and the Church

All those who have embarked on a friendship with Jesus Christ and who seek to grow in this friendship form a community. This community of the friends of Christ has from its earliest beginnings been described as 'church'. The word partly derives from the Greek word *kyriake*, which in turn is derived from *kyrios*, meaning the Lord. Thus it means those who belong to the Lord (Jesus Christ). Hence they are those who live by the Gospel message, celebrate the Eucharist together and shape their lives according to it, especially in the service of their fellow men. The Church is also known as the 'Communion of Saints'. By 'saints' we mean all those who wish to live in union with God, in a personal relationship with the thrice-holy God, especially through the sacramental life of the Church and the Word of God.

Try to become a part of this community of the friends of Christ – in other words, a part of the Church. Make an effort to understand the meaning and importance of the ecclesial community. Try and make contact with your local parish community and to live in and with this community.

Breaking the boundaries of space...

The community of the Church includes believers from every nation on earth. In the Church we tangibly experience the truth that all people are sons and daughters of the one Heavenly Father. Hence the Church is a communion lived in peace, reconciliation and justice among the nations. Thus it is also a sign and pattern for all humanity.

Try to make this universal dimension of the Church a concrete reality in your own life. Try to learn something about the life of Christians in other countries and continents. Perhaps you can find ways of making contact with Christians in other countries. Support the life of the Church, especially in those countries where the true spread of the Gospel has not yet fully taken place.

> *Go into all the world and preach the gospel to*
> *the whole creation.*
> *(Mk 16:15)*

All mankind – indeed Christ actually says "the whole creation"! – is meant to hear the Good News! Throughout the whole world people must be told about it. This is a great mission that has been entrusted to the Church, and it is still a long way from having been accomplished.

... and time ...

Since Christians believe in the resurrection of the body, the Church – the Communion of Saints, in other words – includes not only the living but also those who have died – both the blessed ones who already live with God in Heaven and those who, owing to their sins, must still remain for a time of purification before they are ready for everlasting life with God. There are ways in which you too can actively participate in this communion with the faithful departed. You should pray for those who have died and are still undergoing purification – especially for the members of your own family, who are doubtless still close to your heart. But pray also for all those who have died, especially for poor sinners who during their earthly life were not entirely faithful to God. Ask him, in his great mercy, to heal and purify all their imperfections.

... and all Creation

God, the Creator of the world, did not create man alone to share communion and friendship with him. In the Holy Scriptures we also learn something about the angels – spiritual, incorporeal beings endowed with understanding and will. God in his glory is surrounded by angels who adore him and serve him. The angels too belong to the Communion of Saints, to the Church of Jesus Christ. Angels serve God above all as messengers. The Angel Gabriel, for example, was sent by God to Mary to announce to her the Incarnation of Jesus Christ. And it was angels who told the followers of Jesus of his Resurrection and foretold his return in glory at the end of time.

God is ever present in your life. He looks down upon you from your first until your last moment on earth and cares tenderly for you. He is your refuge and your shelter. He has instructed the angels, his servants, to guard and protect you in all your ways. You may surely entrust yourself to their protection. Entrust yourself to God!

> *Because you have made the Lord your refuge,*
> *the Most High your habitation, no evil shall*
> *befall you, no scourge come near your tent.*
> *For he will give his angels charge of you to*
> *guard you in all your ways. On their hands*
> *they will bear you up, lest you dash your foot*
> *against a stone. You will tread on the lion and*
> *the adder, the young lion and the serpent you*
> *will trample under foot.*
> *(Ps 91:9-13)*

Learning from the saints

You can learn much from the community of the Church. Take advantage of your conversations with other Christians who are on their way to God. Find opportunities to talk with priests and religious too. Look for examples of the Christian life in your own parish.

Learn too about the lives of the great saints. Saints, in the strict sense, are people who have lived their union with God in a very profound way. By the act of solemn 'canonisation' the Church expresses her certainty that these people are even now already enjoying perfect happiness with God.

There is a great throng of saints who have lived their faith in all kinds of different ways and who, in response to the call of God, have each fulfilled a quite specific life mission. There is much that you can learn from them and apply in your own life. Find out about various different kinds of saints and look for parallels and connections with your own life.

You can also call on the saints and ask their intercession, ask them to support you in your own personal concerns or in those of your fellow men. This too is an expression of the Communion of Saints, when Christians seek to help one another, in word and deed, and by asking the intercession of the saints in heaven.

Faithful unto death

From earliest times the Church has paid special honour to those saints who have given their life for the truth of the Faith, for Jesus Christ. They are the martyrs, and they follow their friend and Lord, Jesus Christ, who told Pontius Pilate: *"For this I was born, and for this I have come into the world, to bear witness to the truth." (Jn 18:37)*

Martyrdom is the greatest witness that Christians can give for the truth of their Faith and for Jesus Christ. Even in our times, there is no lack of men and women with such powerful Faith – the countless martyrs of the 20th century, many of whom were victims of totalitarian ideologies, are the proof of this.

Even today in the 21st century, there are still regions of the world where Christians have to endure severe disadvantages on account of their Faith, where indeed they are even persecuted, robbed of their freedom and killed.

> *"Our persecuted brothers and sisters are the elite of the Church. It is a matter of honour that we should show our solidarity with them."*
> *(Father Werenfried van Straaten)*

We have a particular obligation in regard to these, the martyrs of our own time. The very least we can do for them is to pray for them. Anyone who wishes to do more can inform himself – and others – about the state of religious liberty and persecution in the various parts of the world. And finally, we can also provide material help for these persecuted fellow Christians of ours. This too is part of what it means to live in the Communion of Saints, and an expression of the mutual charity that unites us:

> *If one member suffers, all suffer together; if one member is honoured, all rejoice together. Now you are the body of Christ and individually members of it.*
> *(1 Cor 12:26-27)*

Our friendship with God – constantly threatened

> *Enter by the narrow gate; for the gate is wide and the way is easy, that leads to destruction, and those who enter by it are many. For the gate is narrow and the way is hard, that leads to life, and those who find it are few.*
> *(Mt 7:13-14)*

God's invitation to friendship is clear and unmistakable. We have outlined some of the possible aids to living this friendship and helping it to grow ever deeper. At the same time we have warned of some of the dangers that could tempt us to leave our chosen path. But there is no need to travel alone along this path to God; it is much better to do so in the company of other like-minded Christians. Ask yourself if it might not help to talk with others who are experienced in the spiritual life. Find opportunities to talk with spiritually minded people. This can be a great help in living a better life.

And try to play your own part in helping other Christians not to wander from the 'narrow way'. Don't try to hide your belief in the goodness of God. Talk to others about the happiness it has brought you; tell others of God's love! Tell them about Jesus Christ! But be prudent and measured in all that you do and say. Never insist or become intrusive. Take God himself for your example, who waits patiently for our response of love.

> *"We cannot persuade modern man with a paper Gospel, but only if we proclaim the Good News by living deeds of love. No threat of war, no economic crisis, no environmental catastrophe can dispense us from this duty."*
> *(Father Werenfried van Straaten)*

A final word

On the last page of the Bible, in the Book of Revelation, you will find a prayer. In it, the visionary, St John, summarises his longing for Christ to return again in glory and to live once more in our midst – this time for ever. Just as Jesus did, so he too underlines his most important statements with the word "Amen" – not after, but before the utterance. It means: Take note, what I am now saying is most important!

For all the friends of Jesus, for all those who have discovered their profound longing for God and their divine origin, this is perhaps the first and the last, the most important prayer of all. Make it your own and never forget it. May it be the last word that falls from your lips, the final word of your life.

Amen. Come, Lord Jesus!

(Rev 22:20)

A selection of everyday prayers

The Apostles' Creed

I believe in God, the Father almighty,
Creator of Heaven and earth.

I believe in Jesus Christ, his only Son, our Lord.
He was conceived by the power of the Holy Spirit
and born of the Virgin Mary.
He suffered under Pontius Pilate, was crucified, died, and
was buried.
He descended to the dead.
On the third day he rose again. He ascended into heaven
and is seated at the right hand of God the Father almighty.
He will come again to judge the living and the dead.

I believe in the Holy Spirit, the Holy Catholic Church,
the communion of saints, the forgiveness of sins,
the resurrection of the body, and the life everlasting.
Amen.

Glory be

Glory be to the Father and to the Son and to the Holy
Spirit, as it was in the beginning, is now and ever shall be,
world without end.
Amen.

The Lord's Prayer
(Mt 6:9-13)

Our Father, who art in Heaven,
Hallowed be thy Name.
Thy Kingdom come,

thy will be done, on earth as it is in Heaven.
Give us this day our daily bread,
and forgive us our trespasses
as we forgive those who trespass against us,
and lead us not into temptation,
but deliver us from evil.
Amen.

The Hail Mary

Hail Mary, full of grace. The Lord is with thee.
Blessed art thou among women,
and blessed is the fruit of thy womb, Jesus.
Holy Mary, Mother of God,
pray for us sinners
now and at the hour of our death.
Amen.

Prayer of St. Richard of Chichester

O most merciful Redeemer, friend and brother, may I
know you more clearly, love you more dearly and serve
you more nearly.
Amen.

Prayer of St. Ignatius

Lord Jesus Christ, take as your right, and receive as my
gift, all my liberty, my memory, my understanding, my
will – all that I have, all that I am, all that I can be.
To you, O Lord, I restore it, for all is yours. Dispose of it
according to your will; give me your love, give me your

grace – it is enough for me.
Praise to you, Lord Jesus Christ, Son of the living God!
You are the Redeemer of the world, our Lord and Saviour,
who sits at the right hand of the Father.
Come, Lord Jesus, and remain with us, that we may live
always with you and come at last to the Kingdom of your
Father. Amen.

Prayer of St. Francis of Assisi

Lord, make me an instrument of your peace:
where there is hatred let me sow peace,
where there is injury let me sow pardon,
where there is doubt let me sow faith,
where there is despair let me give hope;
where there is darkness let me give light,
where there is sadness let me give joy.
O Divine Master, grant that I may
not try to be comforted but to comfort,
not try to be understood but to understand,
not try to be loved but to love.
Because it is in giving that we receive,
it is in forgiving that we are forgiven,
and it is in dying that we are born to eternal life.

Prayer to the Holy Spirit

Come, Holy Spirit, fill the hearts of your faithful, and
enkindle in them the fire of your love.
Send forth your Spirit and they shall be created.
And you shall renew the face of the earth.
Let us pray. O God, who has taught the hearts of the
faithful by the light of the Holy Spirit, grant that by the

gift of the same Spirit we may be always truly wise and ever rejoice in his consolation.

The Morning Offering

O Jesus, through the most pure heart of Mary, I offer you all the prayers, thoughts, works and sufferings of this day for all the intentions of thy Divine Heart.

Grace before meals

Bless us, O Lord, and these, thy gifts, which we are about to receive from thy bounty through Christ our Lord. Amen.

Grace after meals

We give thee thanks, Almighty God, for these and all thy benefits, who livest and reignest world without end. Amen.

Night prayer

Visit this house, we pray you, Lord. Drive far away from it all the snares of the enemy. May your holy angels stay here and guard us in peace, and let your blessing be always upon us.
Through Christ our Lord.
Amen

Memorare

Remember, O most loving Virgin Mary, that it is a thing
unheard of that any one ever had recourse to thy
protection, implored thy help, or sought thy intercession,
and was left forsaken. Filled, therefore, with confidence in
thy goodness, I fly to thee, O Mother, Virgin of Virgins; to
thee I come, before thee I stand a sorrowful sinner.
Despise not my poor words, O Mother of the Word of
God, but graciously hear and grant my prayer.
Amen.

Introduction to the Rosary

The prayer of the Rosary is a particular form of meditation. In the centre is the life of Jesus Christ. In the 'mysteries' we meditate upon the central events of the life of Jesus and on their importance for our lives. The goal of the prayer is to penetrate ever more deeply into the mystery of Jesus Christ, the Son of God become Man.

At the same time, however, the Rosary is also a profoundly Marian prayer. It was only through the yes, the *fiat* of the Virgin Mary, that the incarnation of God was made possible, so that our Saviour and Redeemer Jesus Christ could come into our human world. Hence every single 'mystery' from the life of Jesus is rooted in the angel's greeting to Mary and her response to God.

The Rosary, precisely because it starts with Mary's own experience, is an exquisitely contemplative prayer. Without this contemplative dimension, it would lose its meaning, as Pope Paul VI clearly pointed out:

> *"Without contemplation, the Rosary is a body without a soul, and its recitation runs the risk of becoming a mechanical repetition of formulas, in violation of the admonition of Christ: 'In praying, do not heap up empty phrases as the Gentiles do; for they think they will be heard for their many words.'*
> *(Mt 6: 7)"*

*By its nature the recitation of the Rosary calls
for a quiet rhythm and a lingering pace,
helping the individual to meditate on the
mysteries of the Lord's life as seen through the
eyes of her who was closest to the Lord. In this
way the unfathomable riches of these mysteries
are disclosed.*
(Pope John Paul II, Apostolic letter Rosarium
Virginis Mariae, 12*)*

Mary was surely the person who inwardly participated the most closely in the life of Jesus. She knew from the beginning of the mystery of Jesus, of his divine origin. She accompanied Jesus on his way, from his birth in poverty and hardship right through to his bitter death on the Cross. Surely nobody can have endeavoured so earnestly to plumb the mystery of Jesus as did Mary, his Mother.

But Mary treasured all these words and
pondered them in her heart.
(Lk 2:19)

That is why we pray and meditate on the Rosary together with Mary, the Mother of God. In her company we contemplate the life of Jesus. Like Mary we too desire to share inwardly in the life and fate of Jesus.

By praying the Rosary, our friendship with Jesus should become more real and vital, our understanding of his divine mystery more profound. We invoke the intercession of the Mother of God in our prayer. We know our own imperfection and weaknesses. Hence we ask Our Lady to pray "for us sinners". At the same time, we can ask Mary to intercede for us in all our needs and concerns and in all the needs of the Church and the entire world. Countless people have drawn consolation and strength from the Rosary, in situations of great need and danger. The Rosary is like a powerful chain, with which we can anchor ourselves in God.

Meditation is strengthened by repetition. Repetition means going deeper, making the mystery our own. And so, for each mystery, after beginning with the Our Father, we pray 10 *Aves*, or Hail Marys, as we contemplate it. These 10 Hail Marys are described as a 'decade' and they conclude with the great prayer of praise of the Holy Trinity:

> *Glory be to the Father and to the Son and to*
> *the Holy Spirit, as it was in the beginning, is*
> *now and ever shall be, world without end.*
> *Amen.*

This praise of the most Holy Trinity is the crown and climax of each decade. It points to the goal of all prayer and to the goal of our entire lives, namely eternal life in communion with the Most Blessed Trinity.

There is a common practice of adding a further short prayer, following this prayer to the Trinity. Possibly the most common and widespread is the Fatima prayer:

> *O my Jesus, forgive us our sins, save us from the fires of hell and lead all souls to Heaven, especially those who hath most need of thy mercy.*

Normally, the Rosary consists of five such decades, beginning with an Our Father and followed by 'Glory be' and the Fatima prayer. Young children and those who are short of time – or who wish to meditate upon one specific mystery, may pray only one or two decades. Even this is a source of great blessings.

The mysteries of the Rosary shed light on various key moments in the life of Jesus. Traditionally Catholics have recited the Joyful, Sorrowful and Glorious Mysteries, and more recently also the Mysteries of Light, or 'Luminous' Mysteries. Christians are free to vary these mysteries and meditate occasionally on other aspects of Jesus's life.

Traditionally, the Rosary starts with the Apostles' Creed, followed by one Our Father and three Hail Marys. Then each decade is recited in turn, starting each time with the announcement of the mystery and followed by the Our Father, 10 Hail Marys and 'Glory be', and the Fatima prayer, if desired. The usual practice after the five decades of each mystery have been recited is to conclude with a prayer to Our Lady known as the Hail Holy Queen:

> *Hail, holy Queen, Mother of mercy, hail, our life, our sweetness and our hope. To thee do*

we cry, poor banished children of Eve. To thee do we send up our sighs, mourning and weeping in this vale of tears. Turn then, most gracious advocate, thine eyes of mercy towards us and after this, our exile, show unto us the blessed fruit of thy womb, Jesus. O Clement, O loving, O sweet Virgin Mary! Pray for us, O Holy Mother of God; That we may be made worthy of the promises of Christ.

The Joyful Mysteries

1. The Annunciation
2. The Visitation
3. The Birth of Jesus
4. The Presentation
5. Finding of the Child Jesus in the Temple

The Mysteries of Light

1. Christ's Baptism in the Jordan
2. Christ's Self-revelation at the Marriage of Cana
3. Christ's Proclamation of the Kingdom of God with his Call to Conversion
4. Christ's Transfiguration
5. Christ's Institution of the Eucharist

The Sorrowful Mysteries

1. The Agony in the Garden
2. The Scourging at the Pillar
3. Crowning with Thorns
4. Carrying of the Cross
5. The Crucifixion

The Glorious Mysteries

1. The Resurrection
2. The Ascension
3. Descent of the Holy Spirit
4. The Assumption
5. The Coronation

I believe – A Little Catholic Catechism

I believe – A Little Catholic Catechism explains and celebrates the riches of the Church's teachings, in the context of the Catechism of the Catholic Church (CCC). Endorsed by decrees from the Vatican, *I believe* vividly captures the essence of central tenets of faith by examining: the Apostles' Creed, the Seven Sacraments, the Ten Commandments, Prayer and the Our Father.

Revised and expanded with extracts from the CCC, *I believe* is beautifully illustrated with devotional works by the much-loved Bradi Barth. Exclusive to ACN, the 208-page book is a must-have for young and old alike, and is ideal for RCIA programmes, confirmation groups, prayer groups and indeed anyone wanting to know more about the Faith. For every *I believe* you buy, ACN is able to send out four to the Church in Need.

© Bradi Barth 2006

Credits

Aid to the Church in Need

Aid to the Church in Need supports the faithful wherever they are persecuted, oppressed or in pastoral need. ACN is a Catholic charity, helping to bring Christ to the world.

ACN was founded on Christmas Day 1947 and is now a universal pastoral charity of the Catholic Church, with thousands of projects all over the world:

- Seminarians are trained

- Bibles and religious literature are printed

- Priests and religious are supported

- Refugees are helped

- Churches and chapels are built and restored

- Over 43 million of ACN's Child's Bible have been printed in 150 languages

- Religious programmes are broadcast

For regular updates from the suffering Church around the world and to view our full range of books, cards, gifts and music, please log on to www.acnuk.org

 *Aid to the Church in Need*

Aid to the Church in Need

In the UK
1 Times Square
Sutton
Surrey
SM1 1LF
United Kingdom

Telephone: +44 (0) 20 8642 8668
Email: acn@acnuk.org
Website: www.acnuk.org

In Australia
PO Box 6245
Blacktown DC
NSW 2148
Australia

Telephone: +61 (0) 2 9679 1929
Email: info@aidtochurch.org
Website: www.aidtochurch.org

In Canada
P.O. Box 670, STN H
Montreal
QC H3G 2M6
Canada

Telephone: +1 (1) 800 585 6333
or +1 (1) 514 932 0552
Email: info@acn-aed-ca.org
Website: www.acn-aed-ca.org

In Ireland
151 St Mobhi Road
Glasnevin
Dublin 9
Ireland

Telephone: +353 (0) 1 83 77 516
Email: churchinneed@eircom.net
Website: www.acnirl.org

In the USA
725 Leonard Street
PO Box 220384
Brooklyn
NY 11222-0384
USA

Telephone: +1 (1) 800 628 6333
Email: info@acnusa.org
Website: www.churchinneed.com